Xtreme Adventure

STORM CHASING

BY S.L. HAMILTON

Visit us at
www.abdopublishing.com

Published by ABDO Publishing Company, PO Box 398166, Minneapolis, MN 55439.
Copyright ©2014 by Abdo Consulting Group, Inc. International copyrights reserved in all countries. No part of this book may be reproduced in any form without written permission from the publisher. A&D Xtreme™ is a trademark and logo of ABDO Publishing Company.

Printed in the United States of America, North Mankato, Minnesota.
102013
012014

Editor: John Hamilton
Graphic Design: Sue Hamilton
Cover Design: Sue Hamilton
Cover Photo: Corbis
Interior Photos: Alamy-pgs 20-21; AP-pgs 1, 2-3 & 8-9; Corbis-pgs 17, 24-25 & 26-27; Defense Video & Imagery Distribution System-pgs 10, 11, 22 (inset) & 32; Getty-pgs 4-5, 6-7, 12-13, 14 (inset), 14-15, 18-19 & 28-29; Midland-pg 6 (inset); National Oceanic and Atmospheric Administration-pgs 16, 22-23 & 23 (inset top); U.S. Air Force-pg 23 (inset bottom).

ABDO Booklinks
Web sites about Xtreme Adventure are featured on our Book Links pages. These links are routinely monitored and updated to provide the most current information available.
Web site: www.abdopublishing.com

Library of Congress Control Number: 2013946156

Cataloging-in-Publication Data

Hamilton, S.L.
  Storm chasing / S.L. Hamilton.
    p. cm. -- (Xtreme adventure)
Includes index.
ISBN 978-1-62403-214-1
1. Storm chasers--Juvenile literature.   2. Severe storms--Juvenile literature.   I. Title.
551.55/3--dc23

2013946156

CONTENTS

Storm Chasing

While other people race to shelter, storm chasers head straight into the wildest weather on the planet. They are brave, foolhardy, smart, and bold. Professionals love the thrills and adventure of their work. But they also know and respect nature's fury.

Storm chasers risk their lives to provide weather updates that help save thousands of people. These adventurers live for that rare moment when a violent storm appears right in front of them and they stare nature in the face.

XTREME QUOTE – It's good to go home alive." –Brian McNoldy, storm chaser

TOOLS & EQUIPMENT

Storm chasers are usually equipped with portable weather stations that include radar to find storms. Many have NOAA (National Oceanic and Atmospheric Administration) weather radios that give constant weather updates.

A sturdy, all-wheel-drive truck provides transportation over rough roads. Maps and GPS equipment help locate the quickest way to a developing storm.

XTREME FACT – *Some professional chasers protect themselves inside a Tornado Intercept Vehicle (TIV). This is a heavy, armored truck. A few TIVs are strong enough to allow chasers to get inside a tornado.*

Cell phones and two-way radios allow on-the-road storm chasers and radar-monitoring meteorologists to communicate with each other. Chasers have cameras and video recorders on hand to document storms.

XTREME FACT – Storm chasers are often "first responders." As the first people at the scene of an accident or disaster, they often travel with emergency first-aid supplies.

DANGERS

High winds, hail, lightning strikes, flying debris, flooding, and inattentive driving are all constant dangers for storm chasers. Even experienced storm chasers can be surprised by tornadoes that are hidden behind thick walls of rain. Their vehicles can be picked up and tossed by tornadoes.

A tornado overturns a car in Henryville, Indiana, on March 2, 2012.

A tornado-driven piece of debris impales a car seat.

Storm chasers face powerful winds that can turn broken branches and other debris into killer projectiles. Adventurers must also protect themselves from blasting hail as large as baseballs.

Perhaps the most dangerous part of storm chasing isn't the storm itself, but the people driving in it. Many people have been killed in storm chasing car accidents. Drivers sometimes talk on the phone or watch a radar feed or a growing storm instead of watching the road.

XTREME FACT – Professional storm chasers Tim and Paul Samaras and Carl Young were killed in Oklahoma in 2013. They were following a massive tornado. It overtook them in their car. They were unable to escape.

Some chasers travel many hours seeking out a storm. They may fall asleep at the wheel. Distracted or impaired drivers are a constant danger. There is also the danger of people fleeing the area. They are frightened and may be driving recklessly and fast.

CHASING TORNADOES

Many professional storm chasers go after tornadoes trying to learn more about how the storms form and how they dissipate. Some storm chasers photograph or videotape the dangerous events.

Scientists place equipment in front of an oncoming tornado in Wyoming.

A scientific instrument measures the wind speed and direction of an oncoming tornado.

Professional storm chasers are often trained meteorologists or atmospheric scientists. Long-time amateur storm chasers also know the warning signs of a possible tornado. Both professional and amateur storm chasers give local radio and TV stations up-to-the-minute information about severe weather conditions.

A Doppler on Wheels (DOW) portable weather radar vehicle owned by the Center for Severe Weather Research is used by scientists to gather information about a nearby tornado.

Joshua Wurman, an atmospheric scientist and inventor of the Doppler on Wheels, sits inside the vehicle. Computer monitors help him track severe weather in the Texas Panhandle on June 13, 2010.

Some adventurers travel with professional storm chasers on tours. These weather fanatics help the pros track developing severe storms and learn how to stay safe in dangerous conditions.

Some inexperienced storm chasers put themselves in harm's way by getting too close to violent storms. They yearn for the excitement of chasing down a tornado. Some pay for the opportunity with their lives.

Members of Tempest Tours hurry to take their last photos after being asked to return to their waiting van as a tornado approaches.

CHASING WATERSPOUTS

A waterspout is a tornado that forms over warm water. Waterspouts are dangerous to people and ships. They may make landfall, and bring strong winds and damaging rain. Storm chasers warn people near shorelines about incoming waterspouts.

Storm chasers in a helicopter watch the intensity and direction of a waterspout near the Florida Keys.

CHASING HURRICANES

Hurricanes form in the warm waters of the tropics. Hurricane chasers are more likely to be in the air than on the ground.

NOAA and the U.S. Air Force have trained "Hurricane Hunters." These government personnel fly heavy aircraft with special instrumentation directly into hurricanes. Winds there reach spiraling speeds of more than 74 miles per hour (119 kph). On board, meteorologists and pilots use training and technology to gather scientific information, as well as help forecast a hurricane's path.

Once a hurricane hits shore, storm chasers on land track the storm's wind speed and path. They note storm surges—the sudden rise of ocean water to greater-than-normal heights that flow inland. Warnings are important.

In 2005, Hurricane Katrina hit the coastal areas of Florida, Louisiana, Mississippi, and Texas. It was the United States's costliest natural disaster and one of the five deadliest hurricanes, with 1,836 people killed.

CHASING THUNDERSTORMS

Thunderstorms are amazing weather events. However, they are also deadly. Lightning, hail, flooding, and hidden tornadoes are all threats found within severe thunderstorms. Storm chasers who go after thunderstorms for weather information, photos, or just adventure must be extremely careful.

Small radios can warn thunderstorm chasers that a lightning strike is about to happen. The electromagnetic charge between the clouds and the ground can be heard on a radio as a loud, intense crackling noise. This warning tells storm chasers to get back to their vehicles or to a safe building.

XTREME FACT – *Chasers follow the 30:30 rule: After seeing lightning, if you can't count to 30 before hearing thunder, get inside immediately. Don't leave until 30 minutes after the last clap of thunder.*

Lightning kills an average of 53 people in the United States each year. Storm chasers see amazing sights and have extreme adventures. The most successful ones know how to protect themselves while helping people and gaining knowledge.

Glossary

ATMOSPHERIC SCIENTIST
A person who studies all areas of Earth's atmosphere, including weather and climate.

DOPPLER RADAR
A special radar system that uses the Doppler effect to measure the location, speed, and intensity of a storm.

GPS (GLOBAL POSITIONING SYSTEM)
A system of orbiting satellites that transmits information to GPS receivers on Earth. Using information from the satellites, receivers can calculate location, speed, and direction with great accuracy.

METEOROLOGIST
A person who studies and predicts the weather.

NATIONAL OCEANIC AND ATMOSPHERIC ADMINISTRATION

NOAA is a United States organization that researches and collects data about the world's atmosphere and oceans and the creatures that live there.

RADAR

Radar stands for radio detection and ranging. It is a way to detect objects using high-frequency electromagnetic (radio) waves. Radar waves are sent out by large dishes, or antennas. They strike an object and reflect back. The radar dish then detects the reflected waves, which can tell operators how big an object is, how fast it is moving, its altitude, and its direction.

STORM SURGE

When ocean waters suddenly rise to much greater-than-normal heights and flow far inland. A storm surge is usually caused by a hurricane's winds pushing on the ocean's surface. A hurricane-created storm surge often causes severe and deadly flooding.

INDEX